JAZZ MASTERS

Django Reinhardt

by Stan Ayeroff

Consolidated Music Publishers

New York • London • Tokyo • Sydney • Cologne

e d c b

Cover design by Barbara Hoffman
Edited by Jason Shulman and Peter Pickow

©Consolidated Music Publishers, 1978
A Division of Music Sales Corporation, New York
All Rights Reserved

International Standard Book Number: 0-8256-4083-0
Library of Congress Catalog Card Number: 77-93736

Distributed throughout the world by Music Sales Corporation:

33 West 60th Street, New York 10023
78 Newman Street, London W1
27 Clarendon Street, Artarmon, Sydney NSW
4-26-22 Jingumae, Shibuya-ku, Tokyo 150
Kölner Strasse 199, 5000 Cologne 90

Contents

Django Reinhardt (1910-1953)

The music of Django Reinhardt and Stephane Grappelli has had a resurgence in popularity in the 1970s. Guitarists as diverse as rock stars Peter Frampton, Carlos Santana and Jerry Garcia, blues great B.B. King, country players Chet Atkins and Jerry Reed, classical masters John Williams and Julian Bream, and nearly every jazz guitarist from Les Paul and Barney Kessel to Al DiMeola and Larry Coryell have expressed their admiration and respect for the artistry of Django Reinhardt. The passion and wealth of creativity in his music will always be immortal. That Django can be an inspiration to musicians of such different temperaments and styles points out the universality of his musical legacy.

Duke Ellington called him one of the preeminent jazz instrumentalists of all time. This tribute to an illiterate European gypsy who told time by the sun, who would just as soon disappear to go fishing or play billiards as keep a musical engagement, came from one of the most sophisticated musicians in jazz history. Django, a man who overcame a severe handicap, the crippling of two fingers on his left fretting hand burned in a caravan fire when he was eighteen, went on to develop an astounding, unique and inimitable technique unrivaled today.

The details of Django's life have been dealt with in many music journals and liner notes to his albums and will not be further expounded upon here. Indeed author James Jones (*From Here to Eternity*) once set out to write a book about Django, who had greatly inspired him. After traveling to France and talking to numerous of Django's contemporaries, he finally abandoned the project because of the inconsistencies and contradictions he found in his interviews. Django will always be the stuff of which legends are made; the real facts can never be known. It is in his music that Django will be found, in all his complexity and simplicity, his fierce passion and soulful romanticism.

Twenty-five years after Django's death, violinist Stephane Grappelli, his partner in the Quintet of the Hot Club of France, is turning on a whole new generation of fans to the joys of "Le Jazz Hot" with his gracious ambience, total musicianship and sublime creativity. At seventy years of age he is an inspiration to see and hear. He cooks with such joy and rhapsodizes so beautifully, totally at one with his instrument, that he bridges all generation gaps. If Django were alive today, he too would most certainly be a force in the future development of jazz.

Yet Django lives on forever on the numerous recordings he made between 1934 and his death in 1953. Director Martin Scorsese is said to have gained his original inspiration for the movie "New York, New York" while listening to the quintet's recording of "Billets Doux" which is featured in the movie.

I hope that this book will help you gain some insight and much pleasure and inspiration from the music of the great gypsy, Django Reinhardt.

Stan Ayeroff
Los Angeles, California
February 20, 1978

Notes on the Solos

"Dinah" December 1934

    This is from the first recording session of "The Quintet of The Hot Club of France."

"Blue Drag" April 1935

"Chasing Shadows" September 1935

"It Don't Mean A Thing" October 1935

    I have transcribed Django's solo and the last section where he "trades fours" with Stephane Grappelli.

"After You've Gone" May 1936

    This has a vocal by Freddy Taylor and features some of Grappelli's hottest playing.

"Georgia On My Mind" May 1936

    This features a vocal by Freddy Taylor. The introduction by Django is superb.

"Shine" May 1936

    Another vocal by Freddy Taylor. Django really cooks on this one.

"In A Sentimental Mood" April 1937

"The Sheik Of Araby" April 1937

"You Rascal You" December 1937

    Django is backed only by the bass of Louis Vola. I have transcribed the third, fourth, and fifth choruses and the two choruses that follow the bass solo.

"Finesse" April 1939

    Recorded under the name "Rex Stewart And His Feetwarmers," this cut featured touring members of The Duke Ellington Orchestra: Rex Stewart on cornet, Barney Bigard on clarinet and Billy Taylor on bass.

"Undecided" August 1939

    This cut has a vocal by Beryl Davis after Django's opening solo.

"Don't Worry 'Bout Me" August 1939

    I have transcribed Django's opening solo and his half chorus after the vocal by Beryl Davis.

"Nuages" (I) February 1946

    This version features Stephane Grappelli on violin. Django starts his solo in artificial harmonics.

"Nuages" (II) August 1947

    This version features Maurice Meunier on clarinet.

"Nuages" July 1950

    This unaccompanied solo was to be part of the sound track for a movie about Django. It is actually a medley of two tunes, "Belleville" and "Nuages." It is an indication of Django's dynamic energy and flow of ideas that this cut runs eleven minutes and fifty seconds. The end of "Belleville" fades out on one side of the 78 record on which it was recorded, and fades in again on the other side, eventually becoming "Nuages." I have transcribed the beginning of "Nuages" with the complete statement of the theme.

Explanation of Symbols

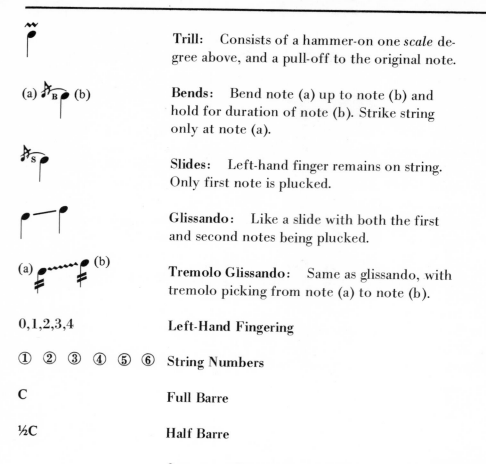

Trill: Consists of a hammer-on one *scale* degree above, and a pull-off to the original note.

(a) **B** (b)

Bends: Bend note (a) up to note (b) and hold for duration of note (b). Strike string only at note (a).

S

Slides: Left-hand finger remains on string. Only first note is plucked.

Glissando: Like a slide with both the first and second notes being plucked.

(a) ~~~ (b)

Tremolo Glissando: Same as glissando, with tremolo picking from note (a) to note (b).

0,1,2,3,4   **Left-Hand Fingering**

① ② ③ ④ ⑤ ⑥   **String Numbers**

C   **Full Barre**

½C   **Half Barre**

Octaves: Octaves are to be fingered as follows:

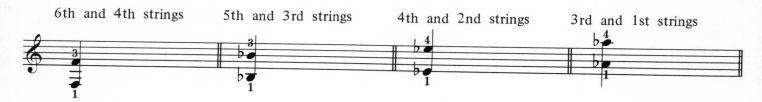

6th and 4th strings   5th and 3rd strings   4th and 2nd strings   3rd and 1st strings

A Note on the Fingering

As I began to work out the fingerings of the solos in this book I was aware that Django used only the index and middle fingers of his left hand for his single-string work. We can only theorize how much use he had of his other two crippled fingers. He probably used them and his thumb in chords. How much? Again, we can only guess.

Keeping this in mind, I set out thinking, "He only had two fingers, so there's not a whole lot of choice." Almost immediately I found myself staring at my left hand, saying, "This is impossible! Django couldn't have used only two fingers!" As I got further along, many patterns emerged and fell into place. They did so only when I used my whole hand.

I have attempted to use those fingerings that were the easiest in producing the desired sound. There were many choices of fingerings; these are only the ones that worked best for me. You may find that another fingering suits your particular technique better than the one I have chosen. If so, feel free to experiment.

It has been fascinating to think about how Django actually played. He must have had tremendous ingenuity and imagination. I did experiment using only two fingers to play the solos, but I found it impossible to do. Therein lies much of the mystery Django has for me: he does the impossible.

A Note on Swing

There are many rhythmic subtleties to be found in Django's music. While either taking a solo or accompanying another soloist Django was always in control of the song's rhythmic drive. Listen to the recordings themselves to hear how Django kept things moving by either adding punctuation to inspire the soloist or swinging madly in his own solo efforts.

In the following transcriptions all eighth notes are to be played in a swing manner. This means that two eighth notes (♪♩) are to be played as the first and third notes of a triplet (♪♩). In addition, four sixteenths (♫♫) are to be played with a triplet feel (♪♩♪♩).

Dinah

Words by Sid Lewis and Joe Young
Music by Harry Akst

8

Blue Drag

Words and Music by Josef Myrow

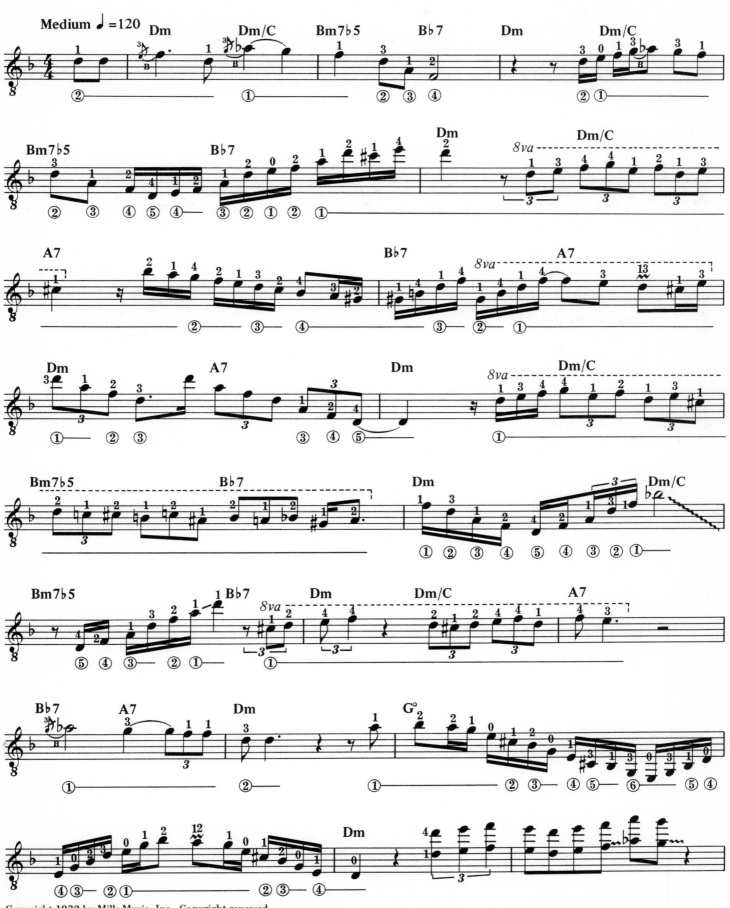

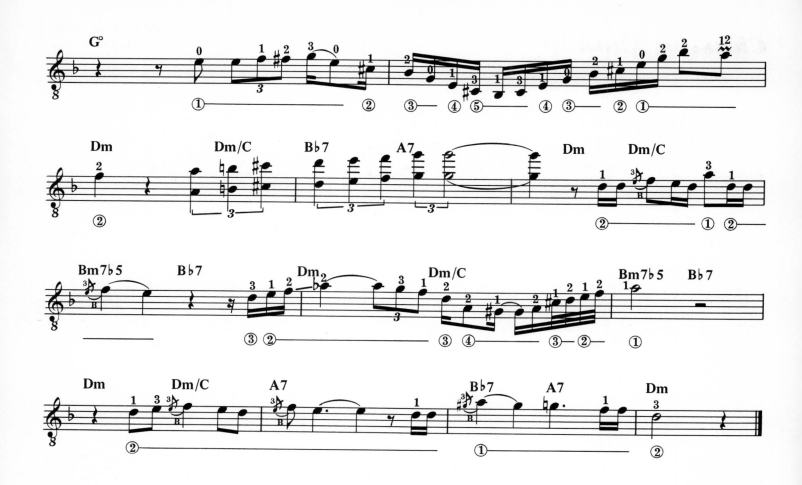

Chasing Shadows

Words by Benny Davis
Music by Abner Silver

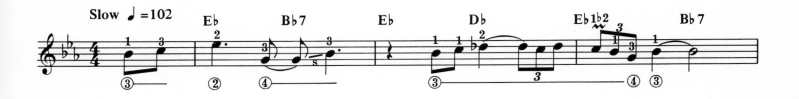

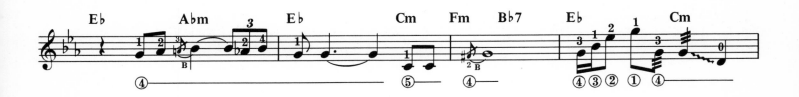

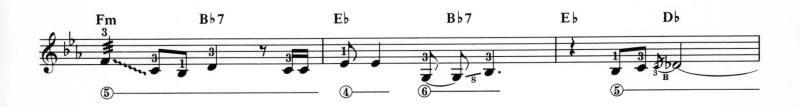

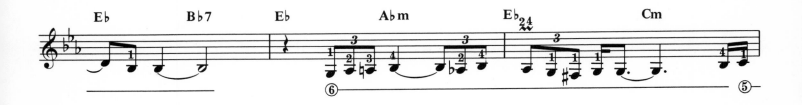

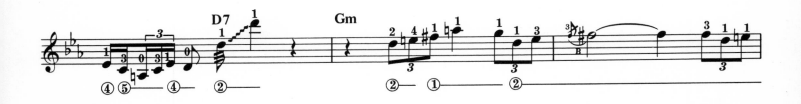

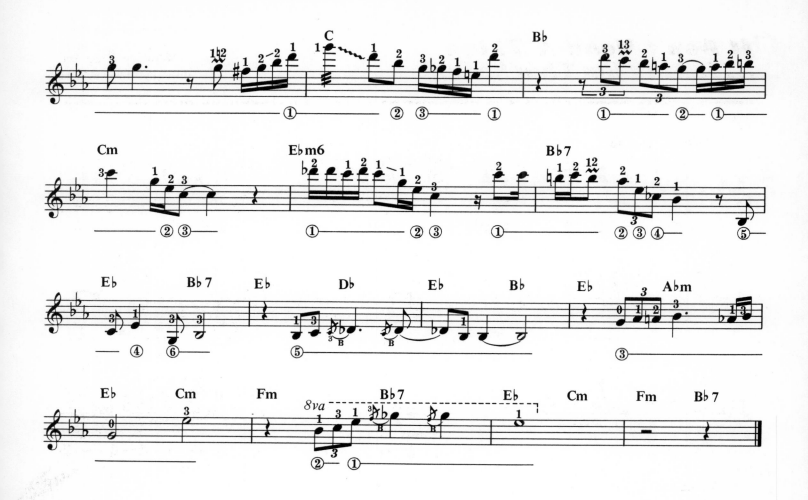

It Don't Mean A Thing
(If It Ain't Got That Swing)

Words by Irving Mills
Music by Duke Ellington

Second Solo
Trading "fours" with violin

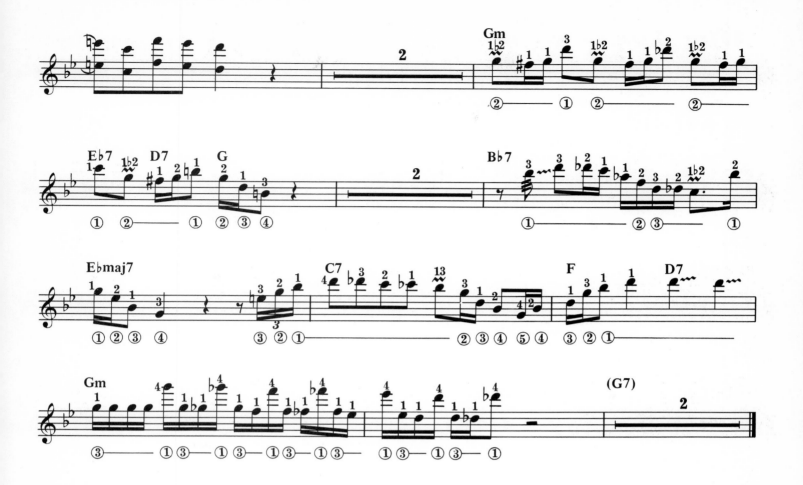

After You've Gone

Words and Music by Turner Layton and Henry Creamer

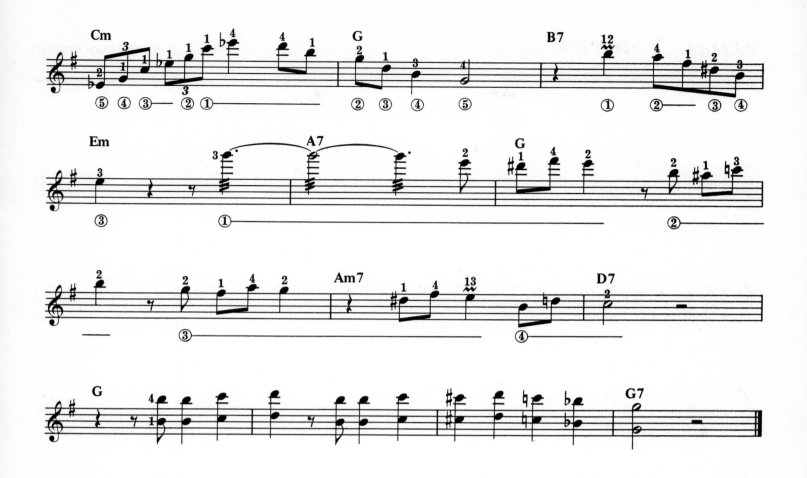

Georgia On My Mind

Words by Stuart Gorrell
Music by Hoagy Carmichael

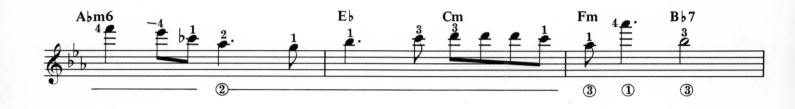

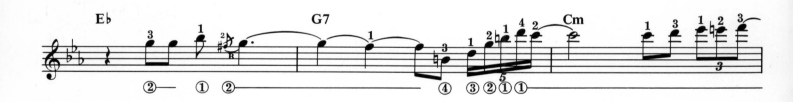

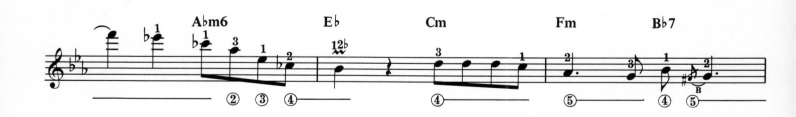

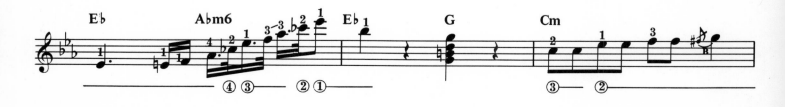

Shine*

Words by Cecil Mark and Lew Brown
Music by Ford Dabney

22

In A Sentimental Mood

Words by Manny Kurtz and Irving Mills
Music by Duke Ellington

The Sheik Of Araby

By Francı Wheeler, Harry B. Smith and Ted Snyder

Finesse (Night Wind)

Words by Robert Sour
Music by Billy Taylor

31

Undecided

Words by Sid Robin
Music by Charles Shavers

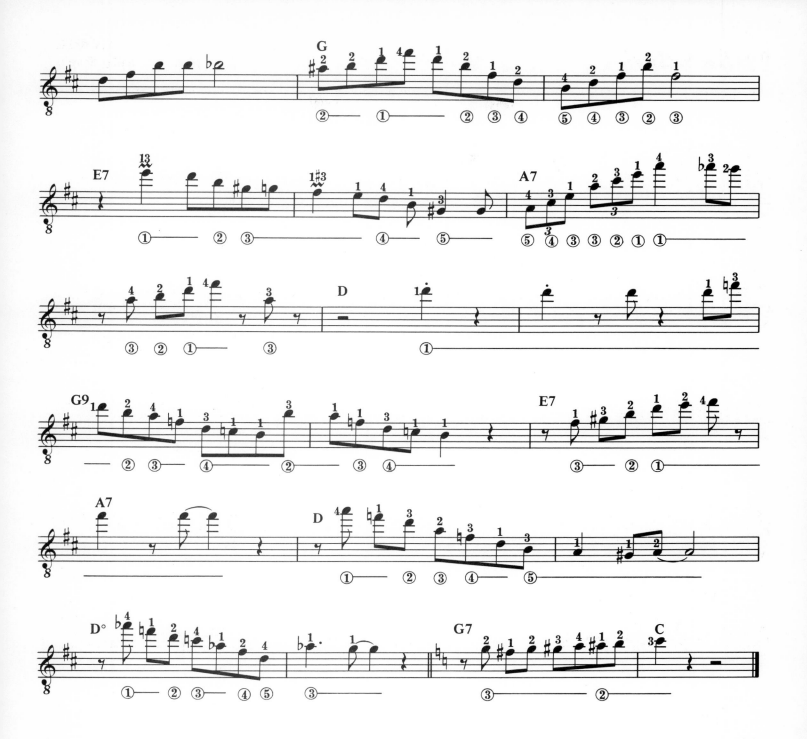

Don't Worry 'Bout Me

By Ted Koehler and Rube Bloom

(I'll Be Glad When You're Dead) You Rascal You

Words and Music by Sam Theard

Nuages （I）

Music by Django Reinhardt

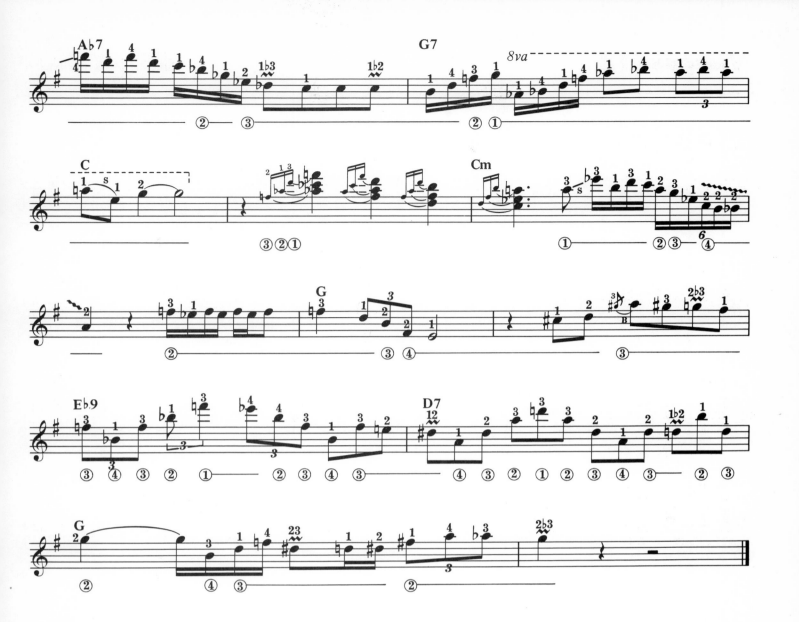

Nuages (Ⅱ)

Music by Django Reinhardt

Slow ♩=100

An Analysis of Django's Guitar Style

Introduction

This section of the book will present the main stylistic concepts of Django's guitar music. Though there is always much to be learned through analysis, keep in mind that there is much that will remain a mystery. There will be notes that will not fit into any analytical category, yet they work. These are what make Django (and all great improvisers) special and unique. It should also be pointed out that Django did not follow any set rules or limit his imagination in any way. He simply played what he heard.

He had the technique to play anything he could think of, and also had an incredible stream of ideas. Though he developed an astounding technique he never used it as an end in itself: he could think as fast as he could play.

Django did have his own clichés, which he would use now and again; but considering his huge output, it is amazing how each solo can stand on its own as special and unique.

Django was one of those musical rareties: he seemed incapable of playing a wrong note. His music never sounded strained or forced, and he didn't have to struggle for ideas. Indeed, there seemed to be so much music and energy inside of him that it had to come bursting out.

Django's Guitar Style

One phrase I use to describe Django's guitar style is "ornamented arpeggio." Though he always had a melodic concept in his solos, he made very frequent use of arpeggios in one form or another. This differs somewhat from the modern developments in jazz and rock music. Today it is more common to juxtapose many different scales or modes to create the harmonic and melodic interest.

You should have a good grasp of the following theory in order to understand the style of Django and his contemporaries. Since it is not the intention of this book to discuss it in detail, I suggest that you fill in any gaps you may have with supplementary instruction or reading.

Chord Formulas

You should have a basic understanding of chord construction (formulas).

Triads: Root (R), Third (3), Fifth (5)
Major (R 3 5)
Minor (R♭3 5)
Diminished (R♭3♭5)
Augmented (R 3 ♯5)

Extended Harmony:
6th chords
7th chords
9th chords
11th chords
13th chords

Altered Chords:
Any chords with a♭ 5, ♯5, ♭9, ♯9

Suspended Chords:
The third of the chord is raised to a fourth.

Chord Family:
Which "family" the chord fits into.
Major (Major 6th, 7th, 9th chords)
Minor (Minor 6th, 7th, 9th chords)
Dominant (Dominant 7th, 9th, 13th chords)

Scales

You should be able to construct and fluently play the various scales:
Major
Minor (Harmonic, Melodic, Natural)
Chromatic
Pentatonic
Diminished
Whole-Tone

Texture and Color

Django's guitar style has three main textures: single string melodic lines, octaves, and chordal passages of two or more notes. This is similar to what Wes Montgomery developed twenty years later. Wes usually started out in single notes, went to octaves, and ended with chords, not often interchanging these different textures. Django employed all these sounds to suit an individual passage, to build tension or reach a climax, all within the course of a single chorus.

Django used two more effects to create a different sound. The first is harmonics, both natural and artificial. Many of his songs end on a chord of three or four natural harmonics at the 5th, 7th or 12th fret. The opening solo to "Nuages" in G is an example of the way he used artificial harmonics. The other effect is the use of the open strings to create unison doublings. "Dinah" (mm. 48-50) is an example of this.

Django was a master of nuance and tone color. It is this kind of personal touch that gives a player an individual sound. Django developed great subtlety on the acoustic instrument that could not be transferred to the electric guitar. His style was best suited to the sensitivity of the acoustic guitar. He extracted different shades of tone to punctuate individual phrases. He had a unique way of ending a note with an upward glissando. Many guitarists do the same thing, but most do so in a downward direction. Rather than attempt to describe the sound of Django's guitar, I suggest that you go directly to the source and listen to the many recordings that are available.

If Django's left hand was incredible, his right should not be thought of in any lesser terms. It was the combination of the two that gave Django his amazing technique. He was fluent with both plectrum and finger-style playing.

Tools of the Improviser

In this section I will attempt to give you some idea of how the improviser chooses what notes to play.

Arpeggios

An arpeggio is a broken chord. Instead of playing all the notes of a chord at once, play them separately, one at a time. Any note of the chord formula is called a *chord tone*.

This makes up the bulk of the musical material in Django's style. I stated earlier that there are not many purely scale passages to be found in Django's solos. What you do find is an abundance of arpeggios.

I am amazed at the velocity with which Django could play different arpeggios. Arpeggios are difficult on the guitar, especially compared to those on keyboard and wind instruments. The key to their execution on the guitar lies in the choice of fingering. I am not sure how Django played them, considering that he generally used only two fingers.

Nuages For Solo Guitar

Music by Django Reinhardt

Major

1. "It Don't Mean A Thing," measure 19

2. "After You've Gone," measure 12

3. measure 16

4. measure 22

5. "Shine," measure 4

6. "Undecided," measure 16

7. measure 31

8. "Nuages II," measure 21

Major 6th

1. "Dinah," measure 7

2. "It Don't Mean A Thing," measure 8

3. measure 24

4. "After You've Gone," measure 5

5. "The Sheik of Araby," measure 21

6. "You Rascal You," measure 4

7. second solo, measure 2

* See section on ornaments.

8. "Finesse," measure 5

9. "Don't Worry 'Bout Me," second solo, measure 8

Major 7th

1. "Undecided," measure 27

2. "Don't Worry 'Bout Me," measure 23

3. second solo, measure 8

4. "Nuages II," measure 28

5. measure 29

Major 6th and 7th

1. "Don't Worry 'Bout Me," measure 23

2. "Nuages I," measure 27

Minor

1. "Dinah," measure 25

2. "Blue Drag," measure 8

3. measure 12

4. "Chasing Shadows," measure 22

5. "After You've Gone," measure 28

* See section on ornaments.

6. "Georgia On My Mind," measure 23

7. "In a Sentimental Mood," measure 11

8. measure 21

Minor 6th

1. "Blue Drag," measure 17

2. "Georgia On My Mind," measure 12

3. measure 15

4. "In A Sentimental Mood," measure 15

5. "Don't Worry 'Bout Me," second solo, measure 2

Dominant 7th

1. "Dinah," measure 28

2. "It Don't Mean A Thing," second solo, measure 7

3. "After You've Gone," measure 31

4. "Shine," measure 21

5. "You Rascal You," second solo, measure 14

6. "Don't Worry 'Bout Me," measure 21

7. "Nuages I," measure 22

Dominant 9th

1. "Dinah," measure 9

2. measure 27

3. measure 41

4. "After You've Gone," measure 9

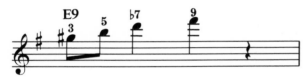

5. "Undecided," measure 1

6. measure 11

7. "Nuages I," measure 17

13th Chords

1. "After You've Gone," measure 10

2. "Don't Worry 'Bout Me," second solo, measure 7

3. "Nuages I," measure 6

4. "Nuages II," measure 2

5. measure 22

*See section on Connecting Chord Tones.

Altered Dominant and Diminished Chords

1. "Blue Drag," measure 7

2. measure 22

3. "It Don't Mean A Thing," second solo, measure 6

4. "Undecided," measure 14

5. "Nuages I," measure 22

6. "Nuages II," measure 3

7. measure 10

8. measure 23

Connecting Chord Tones

There are three basic ways to connect chord tones:

Chord Tone to Chord Tone

This means simply moving directly from one chord tone to another. All arpeggios fall into this category.

Scalewise

You may fill in the notes of the scale between two chord tones. The notes between chord tones are called *passing tones* (PT). Note that it is most common for passing tones to fall on a weak beat or the weak part of a beat. Chord tones usually fall on the strong beat or strong part of a beat.

Scalewise Passing Tones (PT)

1. "Dinah," measure 16

2. measure 61

3. "Georgia On My Mind," measure 3

4. "The Sheik of Araby," measure 16

5. "You Rascal You," measure 14

6. "Finesse," measure 9

7. measure 13

8. "Undecided," measure 35

Chromatically

You may play the notes of the chromatic scale between any two chord tones. The most common are:

> root to ♭7th (see examples 2,3,4,8)
> 3rd to 9th (see examples 1,3,4,8)

Also common are:

> 3rd to 5th (examples 9,10)
> 5th to 3rd (examples 6,7)
> 5th to ♭7th (example 5)
> 9th to 3rd (example 5)
> 9th to root (example 3)
> root to 9th (example 5)

Passing tones frequently lead from a chord tone of one chord to a chord tone of another. See example 3, in which the root of an A minor chord descends chromatically to F♯, the third of a D major chord.

Chromatic Passing Tones

1. "It Don't Mean a Thing," measure 9

2. "Shine," measure 11

3. measure 13

4. measure 41

5. measure 53

6. "The Sheik of Araby," measure 4

7. "You Rascal You," measure 8

8. "Undecided," measure 29

9. "Don't Worry 'Bout Me," measure 20

10. second solo, measure 5

Chromatic Glissando

Django used the chromatic glissando with great effect. It is amazing how he executed them so perfectly. He coordinated his left hand and his right hand in such a way that each time he picked the string he would move one fret. At the same time, he was doing a tremendously fast tremolo with his right hand.

The use of four half-steps descending in this manner occurs frequently in Django's music.

58

Chromatic Glissando (four half - steps)

1. "After You've Gone," measure 24

2. "Shine," measure 5

3. "The Sheik of Araby," measure 24

4. "You Rascal You," measure 6

5. measure 10

6. Second solo, measure 13

7. Second solo, measure 28

8. "Nuages I," measure 7

Chromatic Glissando (long)

Django also used the chromatic glissando over very long intervals.

1. "Chasing Shadows," measure 7

2. measure 16

3. measure 20

4. "Georgia On My Mind," measure 22

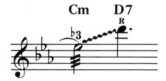

5. "Shine," measure 21

6. "In a Sentimental Mood," measure 35

7. "The Sheik of Araby," measure 17

8. "Don't Worry 'Bout Me," second solo, measure 1

60

Combined Scale and Chromatic Passing Tones

Additionally, any combination of the previous three methods may be used. This is something Django did a great deal.

1. "Georgia On My Mind," measure 11

2. "In A Sentimental Mood," measure 34

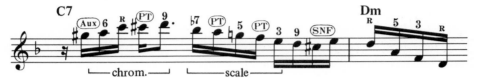

3. measure 36

4. "The Sheik of Araby," measure 1

5. measure 15

6. "Don't Worry 'Bout Me," measure 4

7. measure 30

8. "Nuages II," measure 6

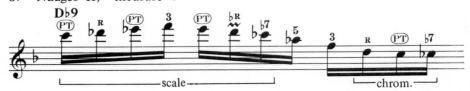

Ornaments

Django created additional interest by playing around the basic chord tones in several different ways.

The Trill (∿)

This figure means to play the chord tone first, then hammer-on one scale degree above the chord tone, then pull-off to the chord tone again. An accidental above the trill sign means that the scale degree above the chord tone is altered. It will still be either a half step or a whole step above the original chord tone.

1. "Chasing Shadows," measure 3

2. "After You've Gone," measure 8

3. "Shine," measure 6

4. "The Sheik of Araby," measure 5

5. "Finesse," measure 10

6. "Undecided," measure 1

7. measure 29

8. "Nuages II," measure 28

Bending Notes (B)

Django only used bends of a half step. He would approach a chord tone from a half step below it, and bend that note until it sounded like the chord tone. He used the bend on any chord tone.

1. "Blue Drag," measure 1

2. "Chasing Shadows," measure 4

3. measure 18

4. "It Don't Mean A Thing," measure 2

5. "After You've Gone," measure 4

6. "Georgia On My Mind," measure 9

7. measure 17

8. "The Sheik of Araby," measure 14

9. measure 27

10. "Don't Worry 'Bout Me," measure 1

11. measure 31

Auxiliary Tones (Aux)

This ornaments a stationary chord tone by playing a half or a whole step above or below any chord tone, and then returning to the original tone. The chord tone needn't always be played first.

1. "Dinah," measure 23

2. "It Don't Mean A Thing," measure 4

3. measure 24

4. second solo, measure 8

5. "Shine," measure 28

6. "Undecided," measure 9

7. measure 27

8. "Nuages I," measure 13

9. "Nuages II," measure 11

10. measure 29

Surrounding Note Figure (SNF)

There is one combination used by Django that I call the *Surrounding Note Figure* (SNF). It consists of playing a half step below and one *scale degree* above any chord tone. Frequently the chord tone itself appears between the two notes of the surrounding note figure.

1. "Dinah," measure 38

2. "It Don't Mean A Thing," measure 17

3. "After You've Gone," measure 32

4. "Georgia On My Mind," measure 3

5. "Shine," measure 23

6. "In A Sentimental Mood," measure 13

7. "You Rascal You," second solo, measure 17

67

8. "Don't Worry 'Bout Me," measure 24

9. "Nuages II," measure 5

10. measure 8

11. measure 12

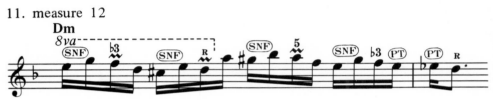

Anticipation (Ant)

The connecting figure or arpeggio often anticipates the next chord change: this gives momentum to a solo. Django always knew where he was going, and you should too. Don't get hung up on bar lines. To construct a longer melodic line you must plan ahead. Suppose you have a measure in G followed by one beginning with an Eb 7 chord. Don't just think of four beats of G, stop at the bar line, and begin to think of four beats of Eb7. This will inhibit a smooth progression of ideas and produce too many short, choppy phrases. Try to link your ideas together through various chord changes by using a repeated figure or riff, altering the scale so it fits the next chord change, playing tones common to both chords, or anticipating the next chord change. Keeping the momentum going by connecting phrases in a flowing manner is essential to good improvisation.

1. "Dinah," measure 10

2. measure 40

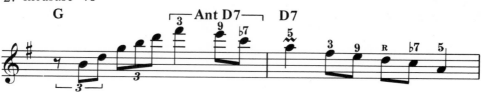

3. "It Don't Mean A Thing," measure 4

4. measure 10

5. measure 16

6. "After You've Gone," measure 29

69

7. "The Sheik of Araby," measure 3

8. "You Rascal You," measure 30

9. "Undecided," measure 34

10. "Nuages I," measure 15

Discography

The following is a discography of the solos I have transcribed in this book. These albums are still in print and are available in most record stores that have a selection of vintage jazz.

Djangologie 2	(Pathe 2CO54-16002)	"After You've Gone" "Georgia On My Mind" "Shine"
Djangologie 3	(Pathe 2CO54-16003)	"In A Sentimental Mood" "The Sheik Of Araby" ✔
Djangologie 7	(Pathe 2CO54-16007)	"You Rascal You"
Djangologie 8	(Pathe 2CO54-16008)	"Finesse"
Djangologie 18	(Pathe 2CO54-16018)	"Nuages" (for unaccompanied guitar solo)
Django 1934	(Vogue CLD 745)	"Dinah" ✔ "Blue Drag"
Django Reinhardt	(Archive Of Jazz FS 212)	"Nuages" (in F)
Django Reinhardt Memorial Album Vol. 3	(Period SPL 1203)	"Nuages" (in F)
Django Reinhardt— Stephane Grappelly With The Quintet of The Hot Club of France	(GNP-Crescendo GNP-9001)	"Nuages" (starts in harmonics in G)
Parisian Swing	(GNP-Crescendo GNP-9002)	"Chasing Shadows" "Undecided" "Don't Worry 'Bout Me"
Django 1935-1939	(GNP-Crescendo GNP-9019)	"It Don't Mean A Thing"
Django 1935	(GNP-Crescendo GNP-9023)	"Chasing Shadows"
Django 1934	(GNP-Crescendo GNP-9031)	"Dinah" Blue Drag"